I0464630

Color Him Mine

Instant Boyfriend

(Just Add Color)

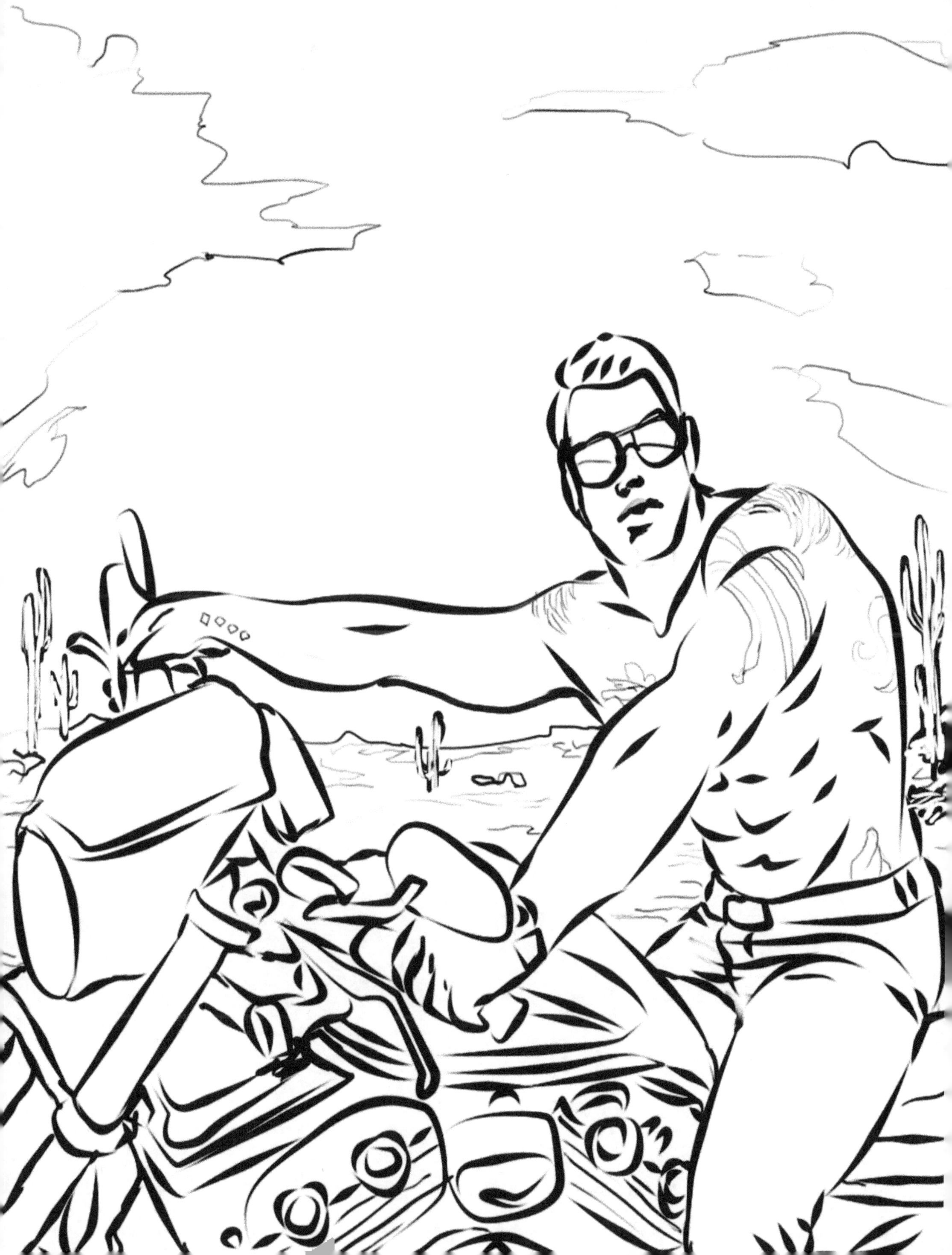

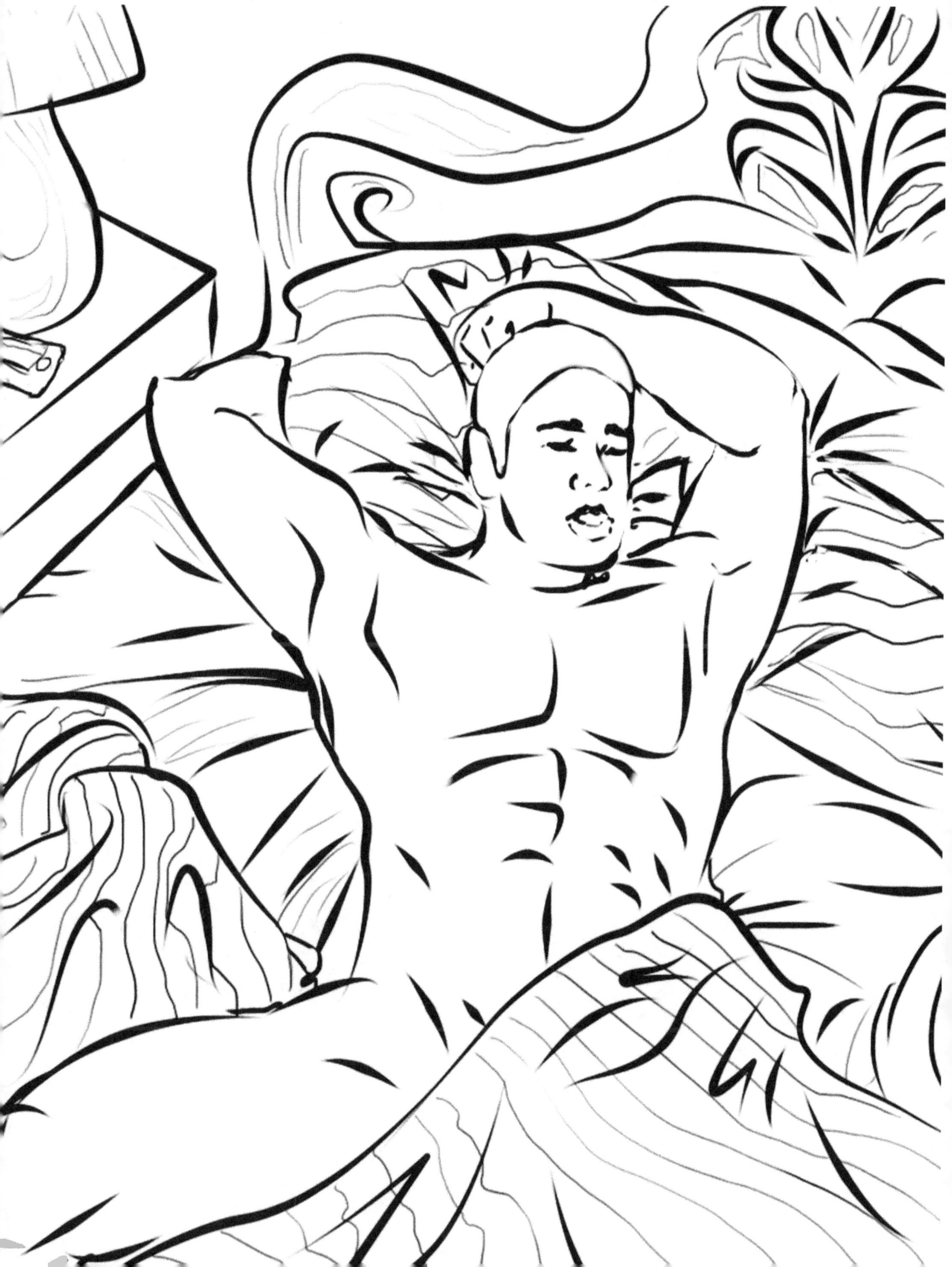

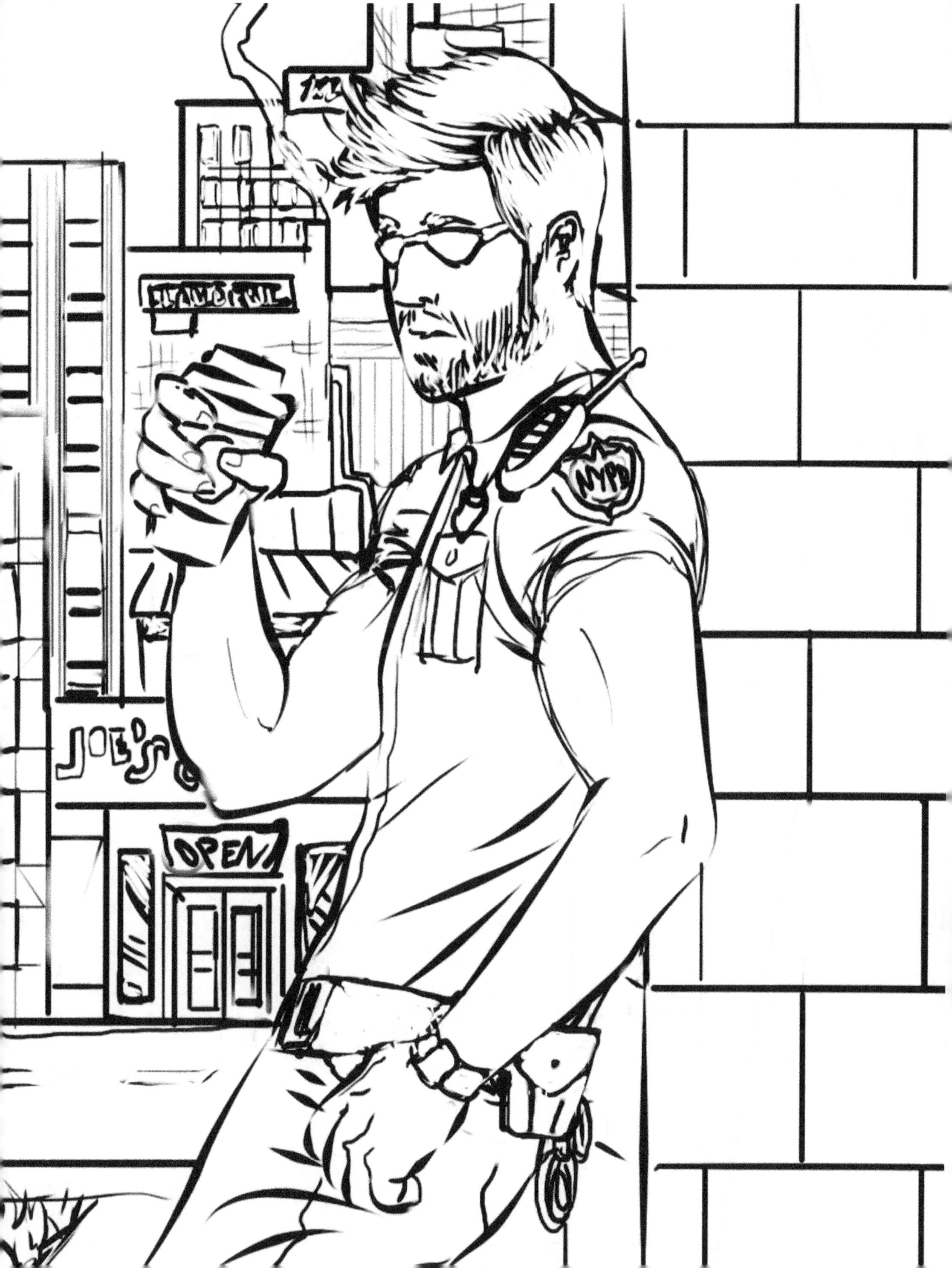
NYPD
JOE'S
OPEN

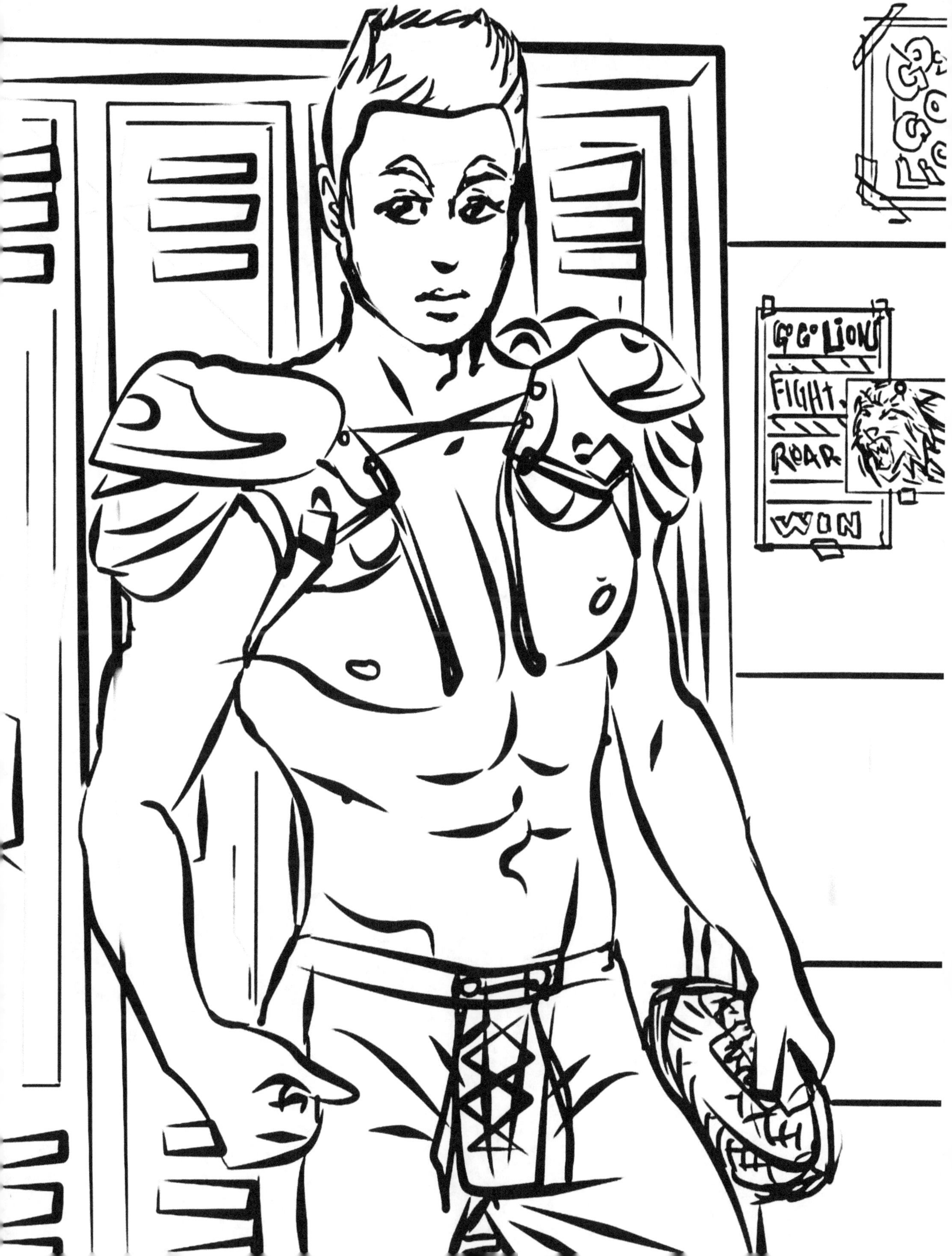
GO GO LIONS
FIGHT
ROAR
WIN

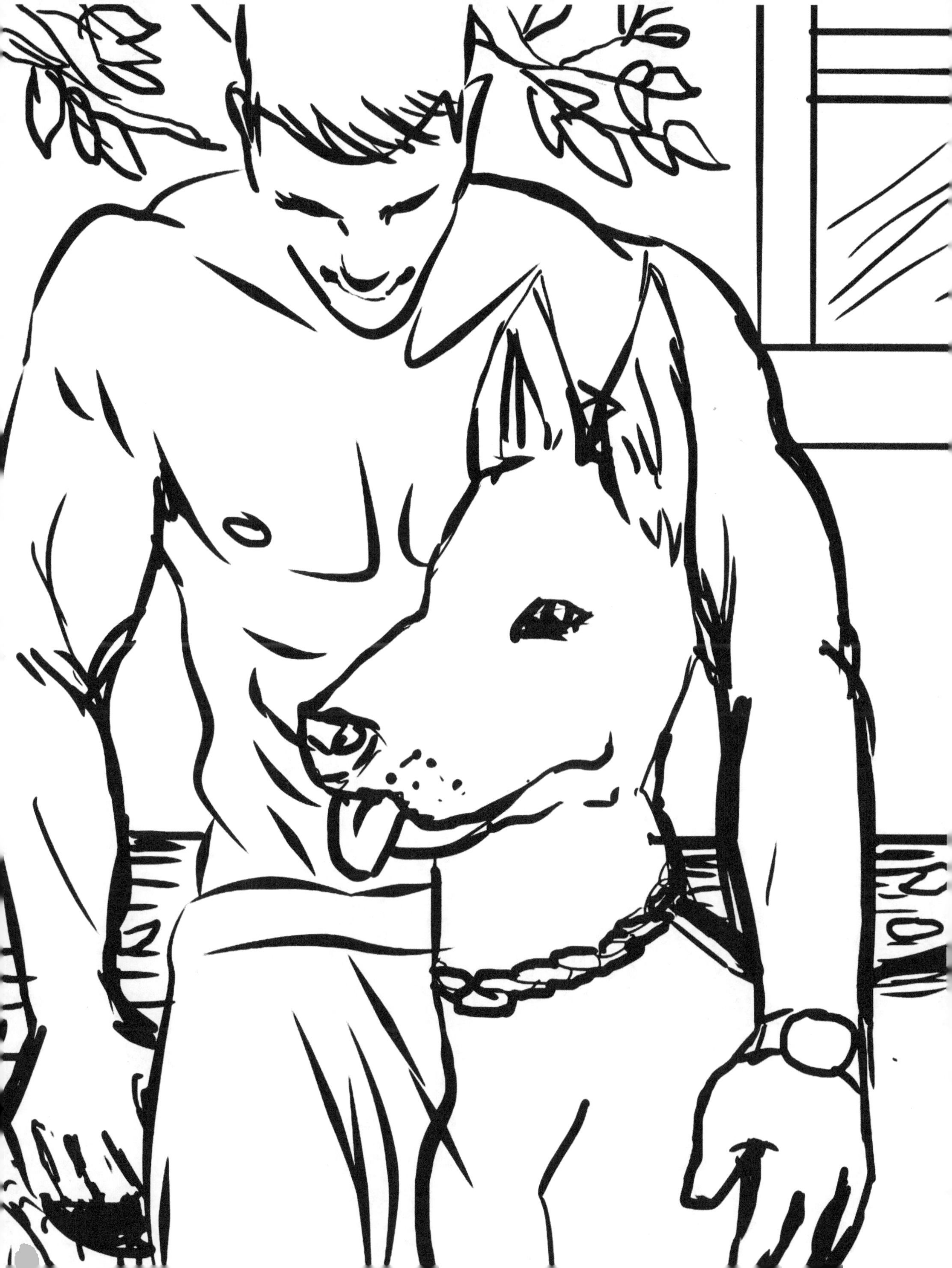

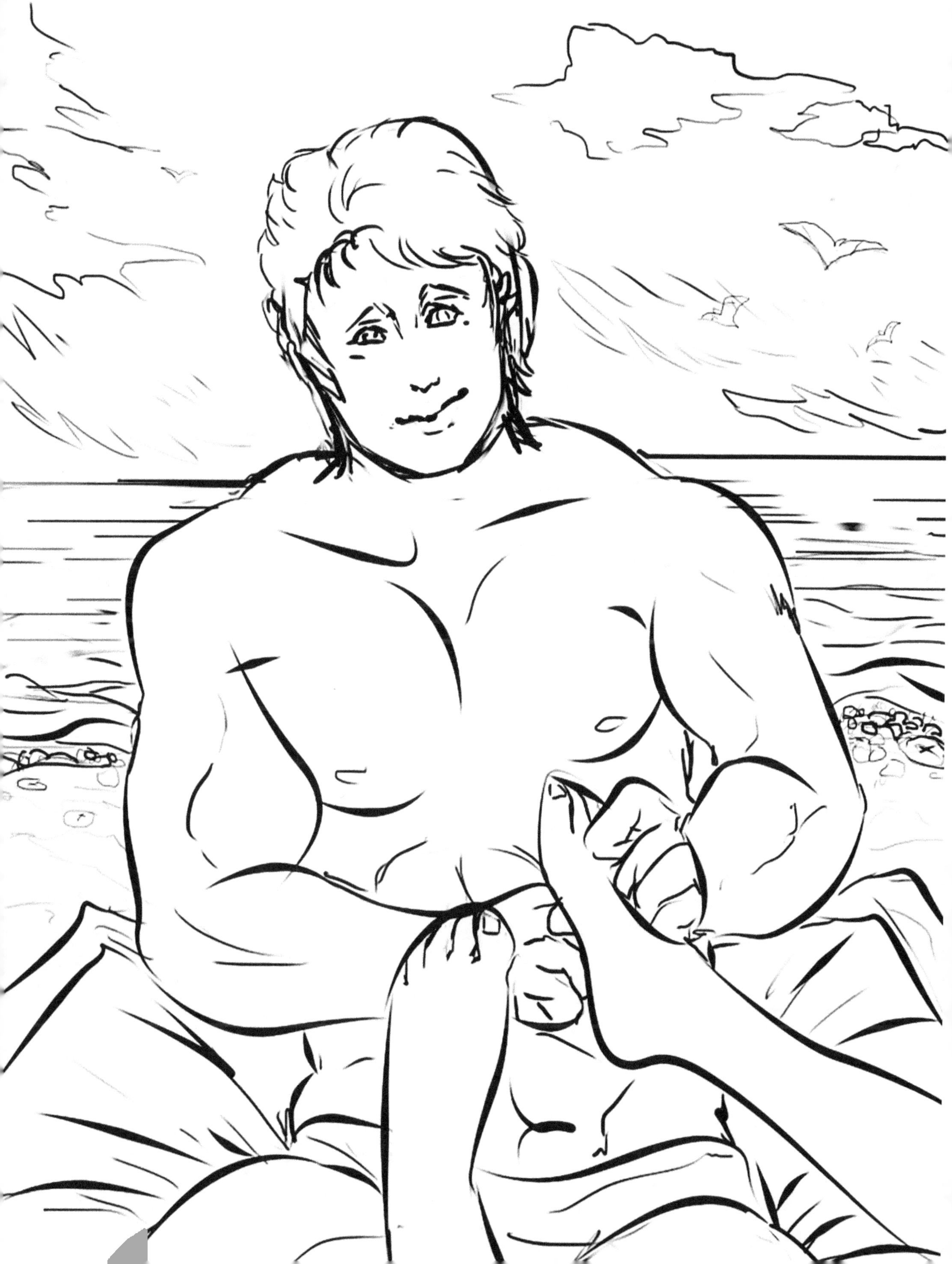

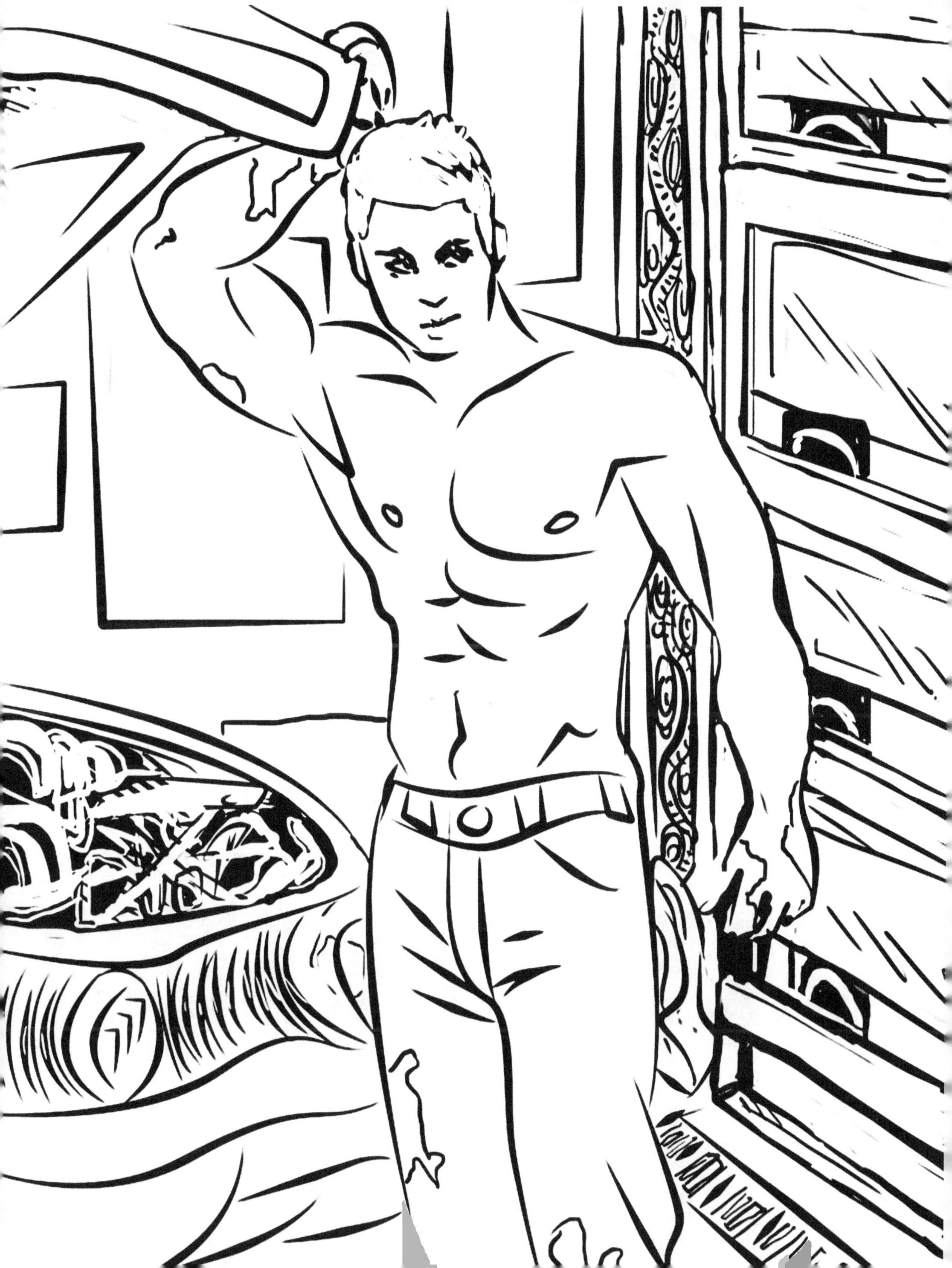

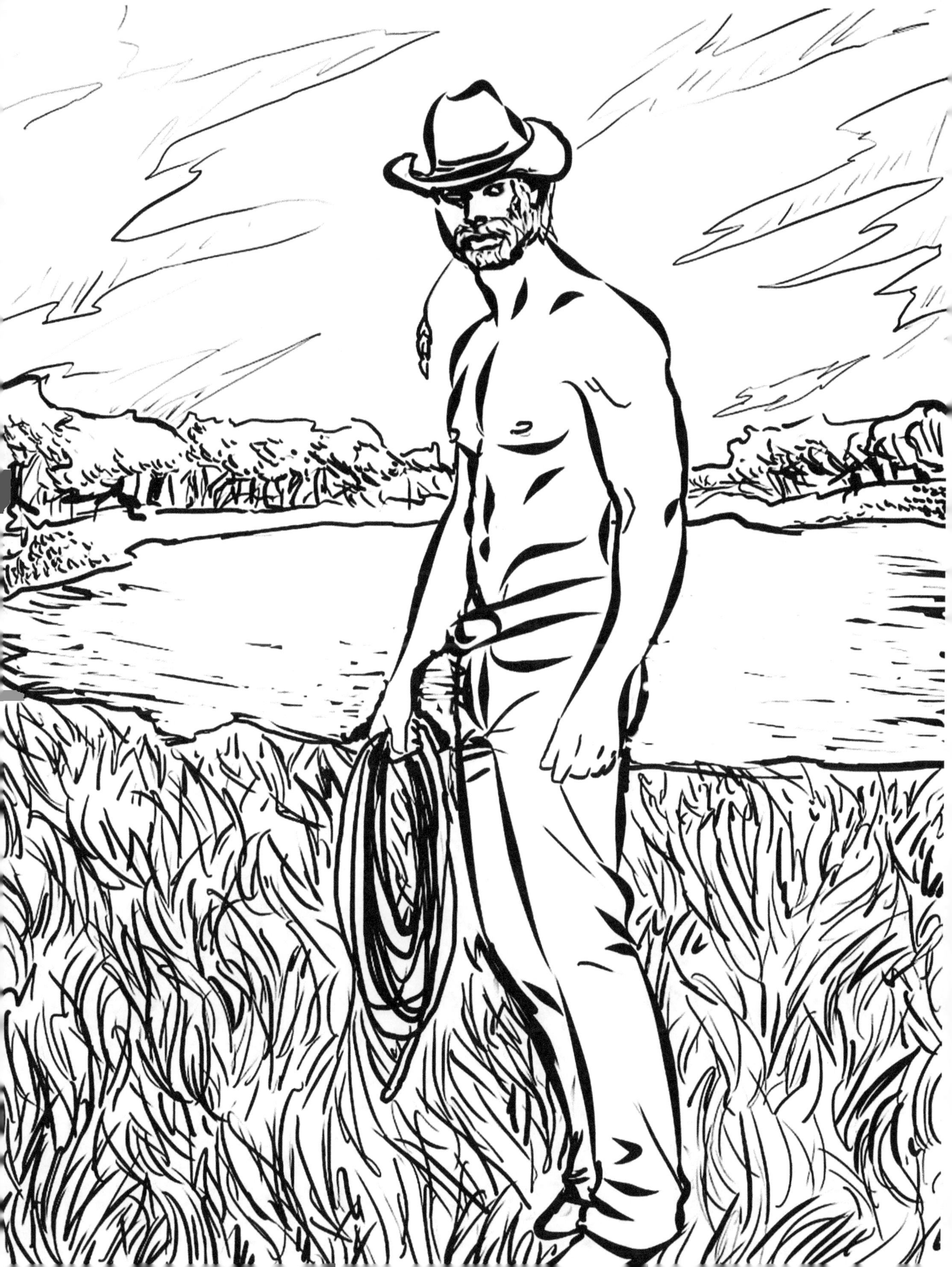

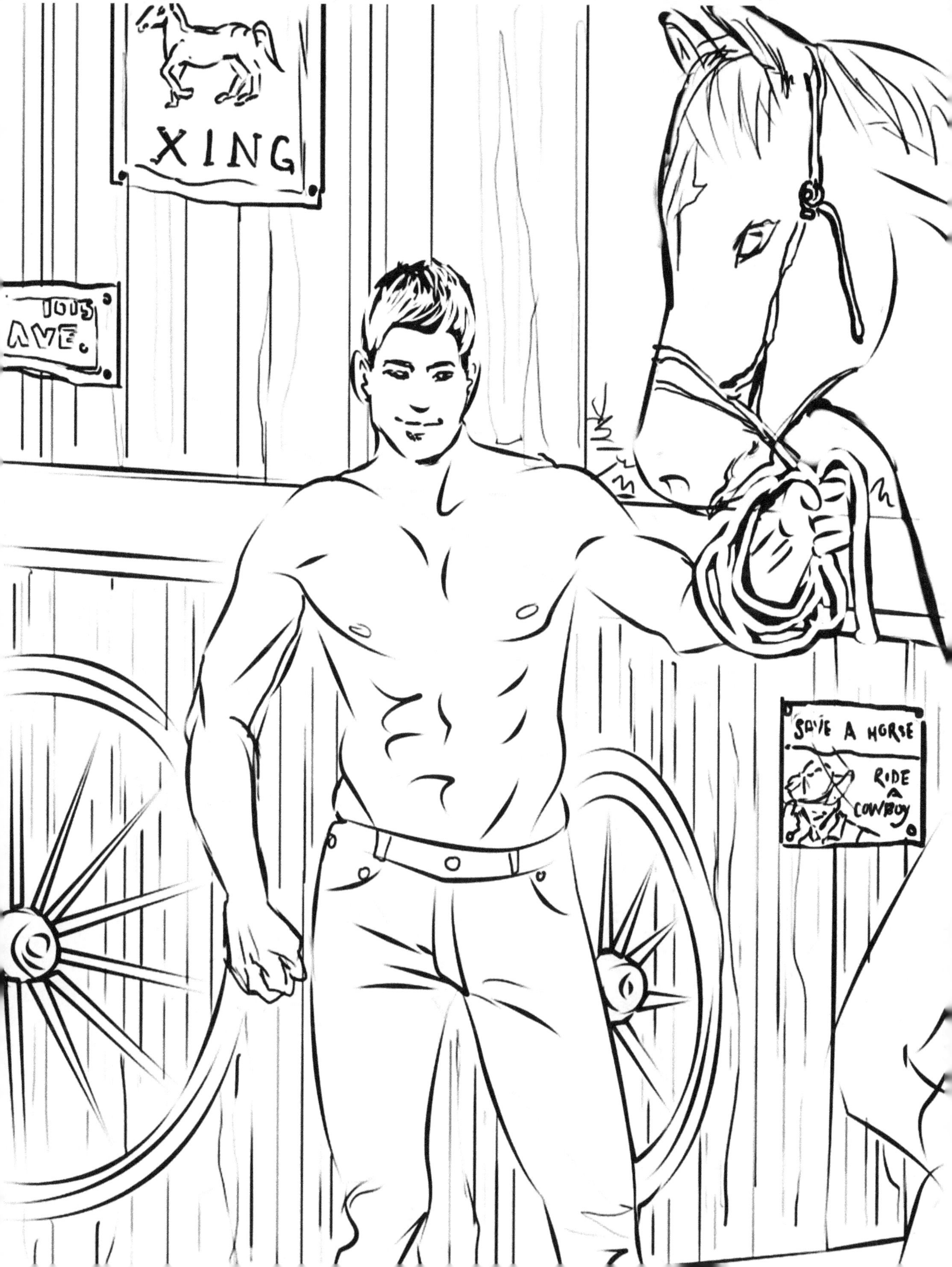
XING
1015
AVE.
SAVE A HORSE
RIDE A COWBOY

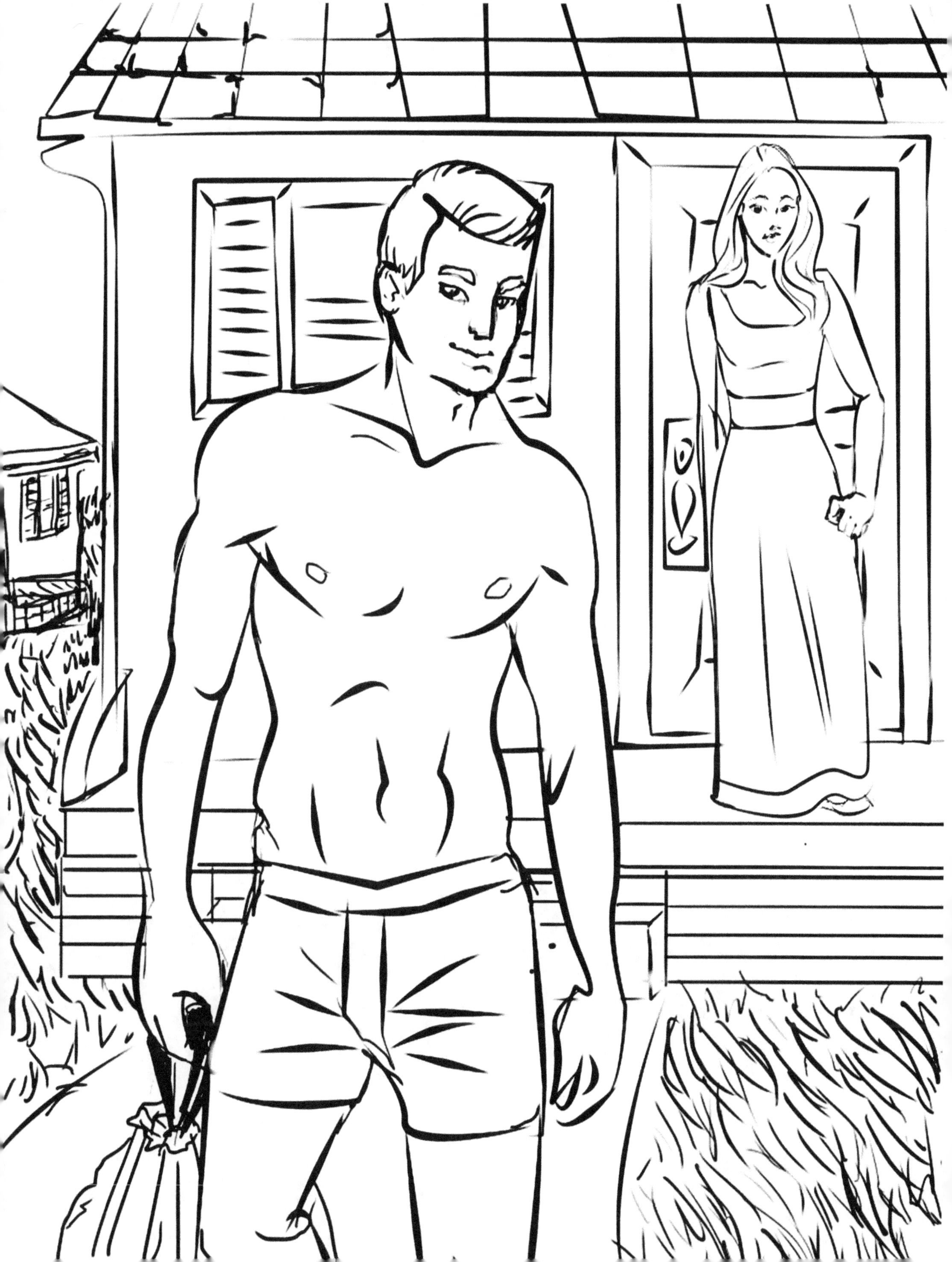

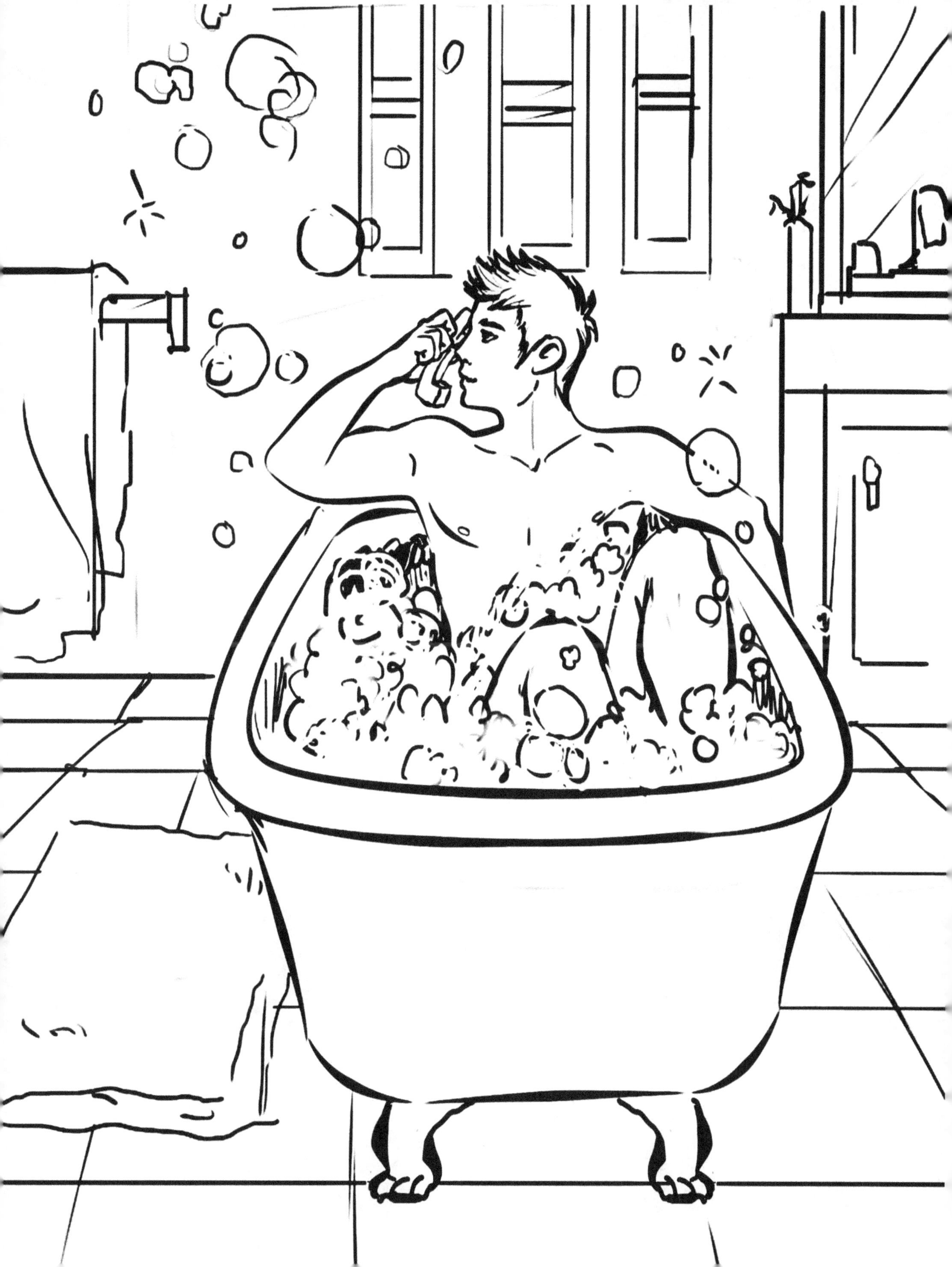

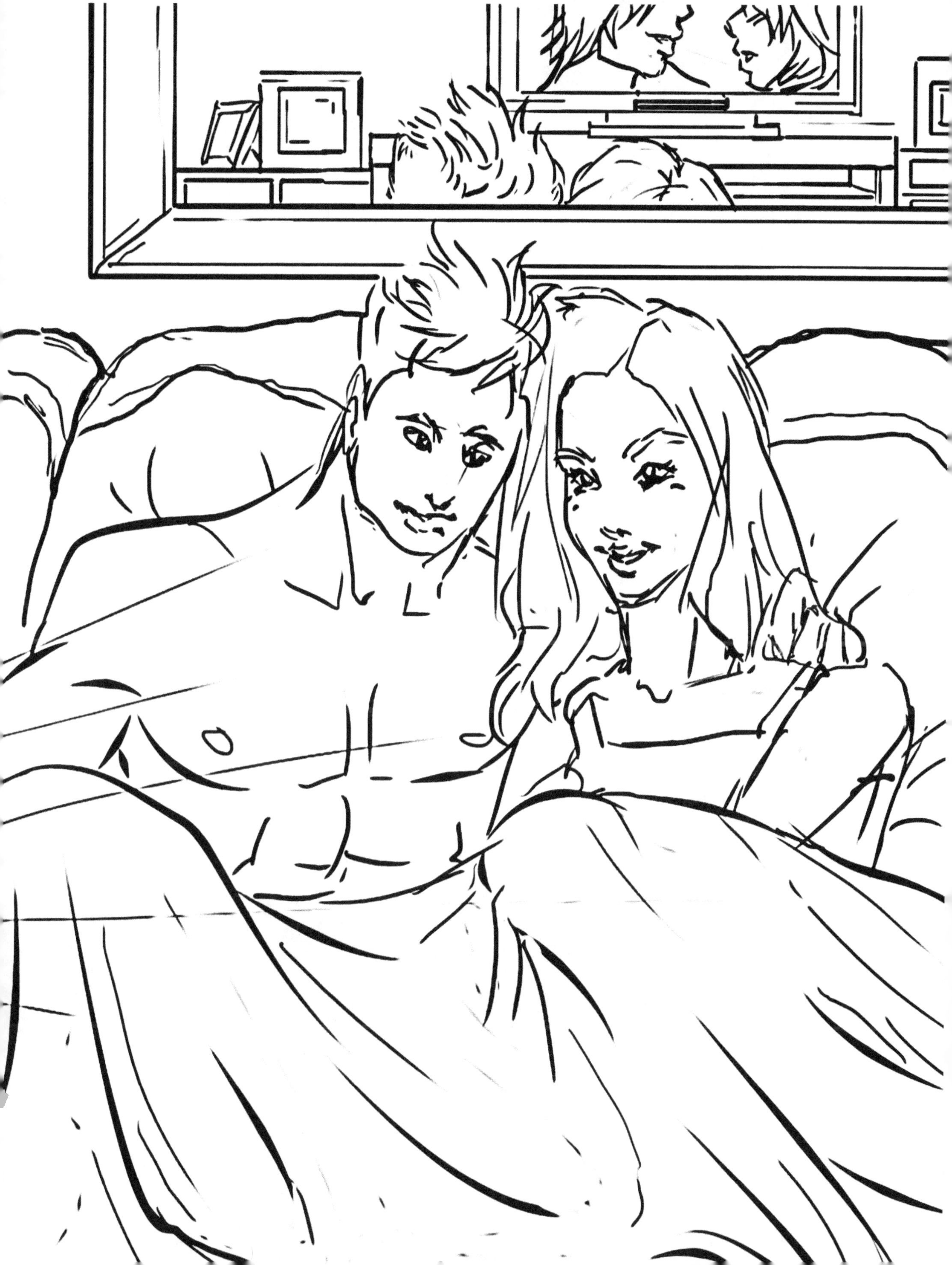

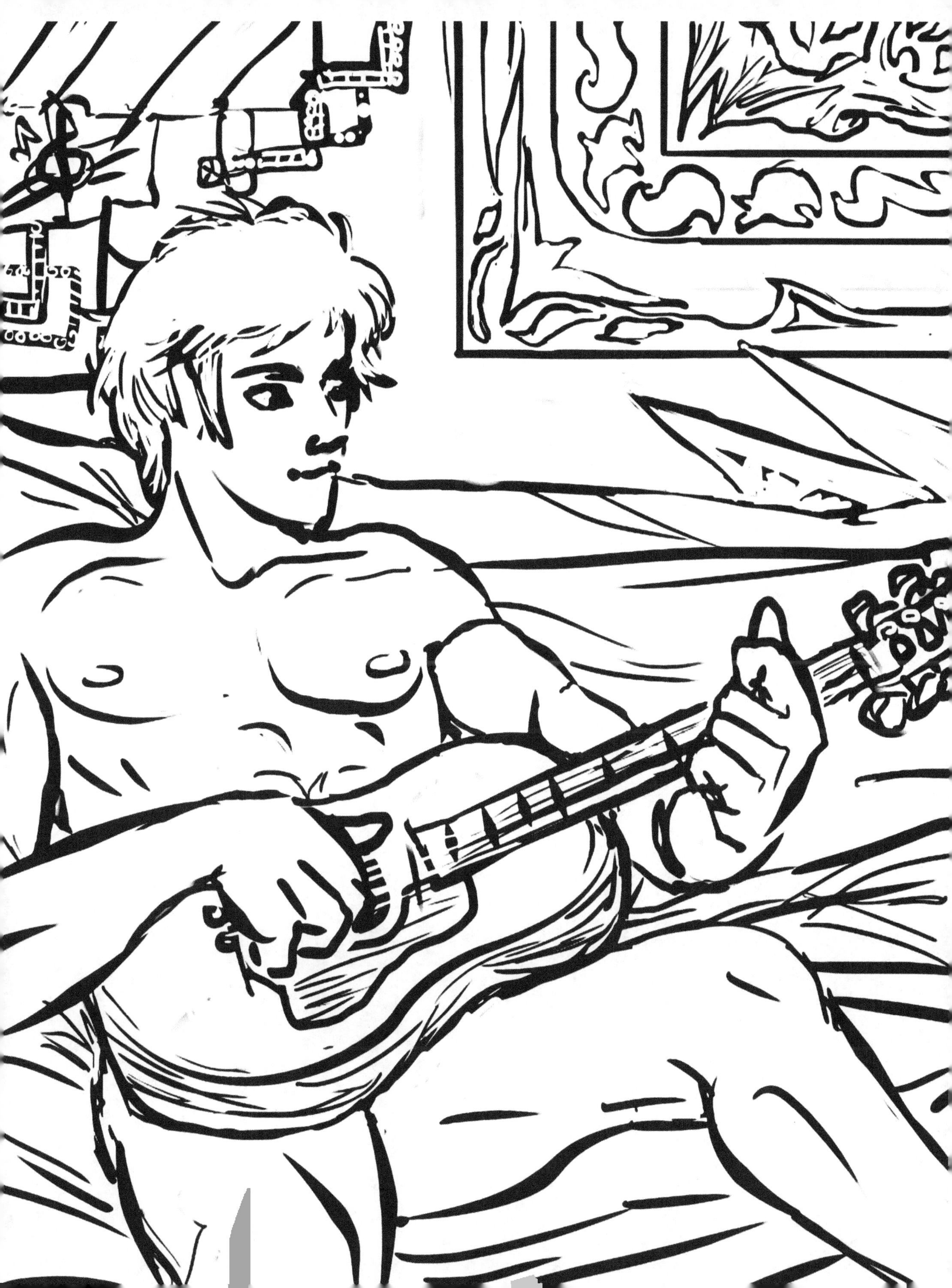

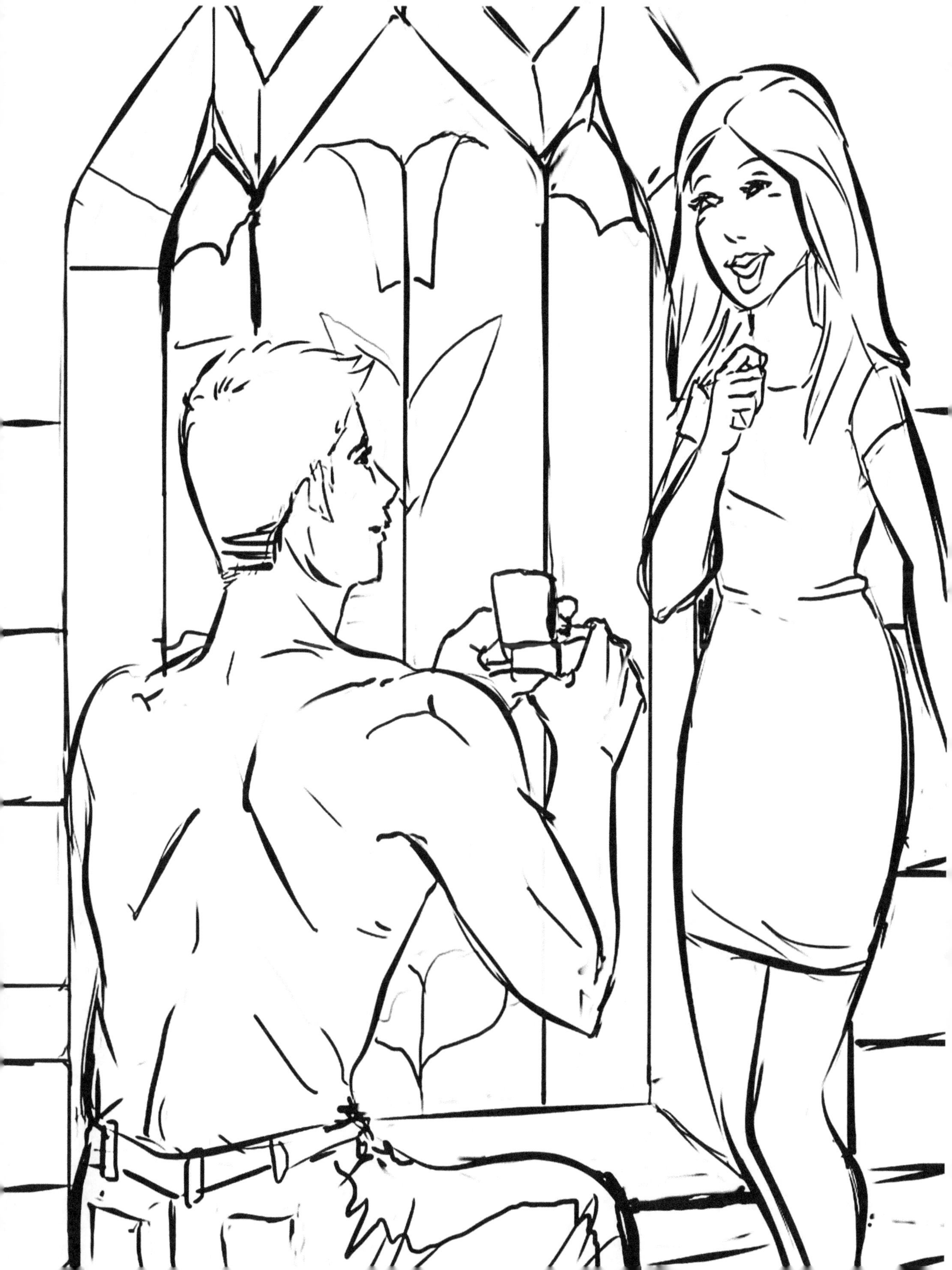

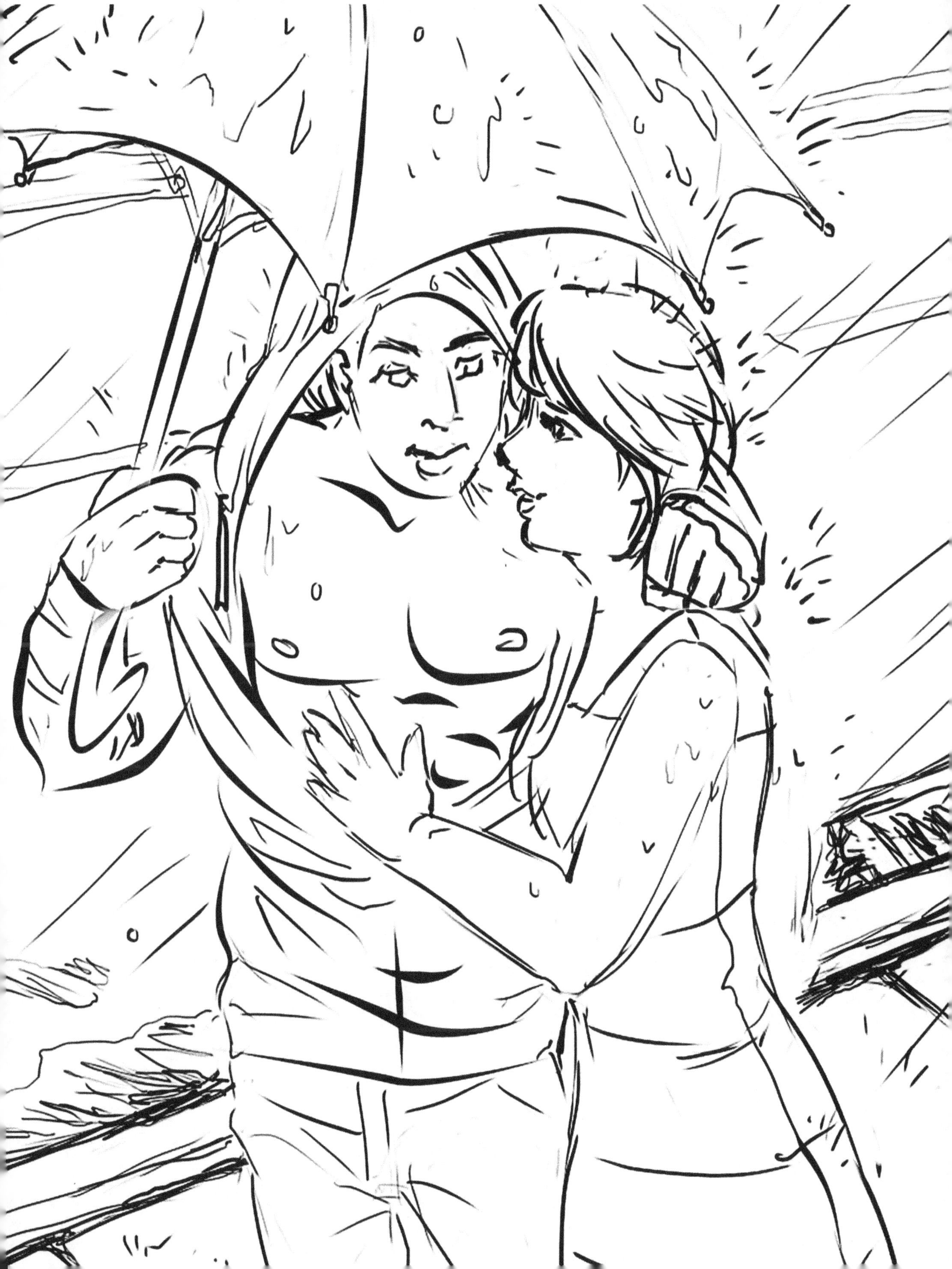

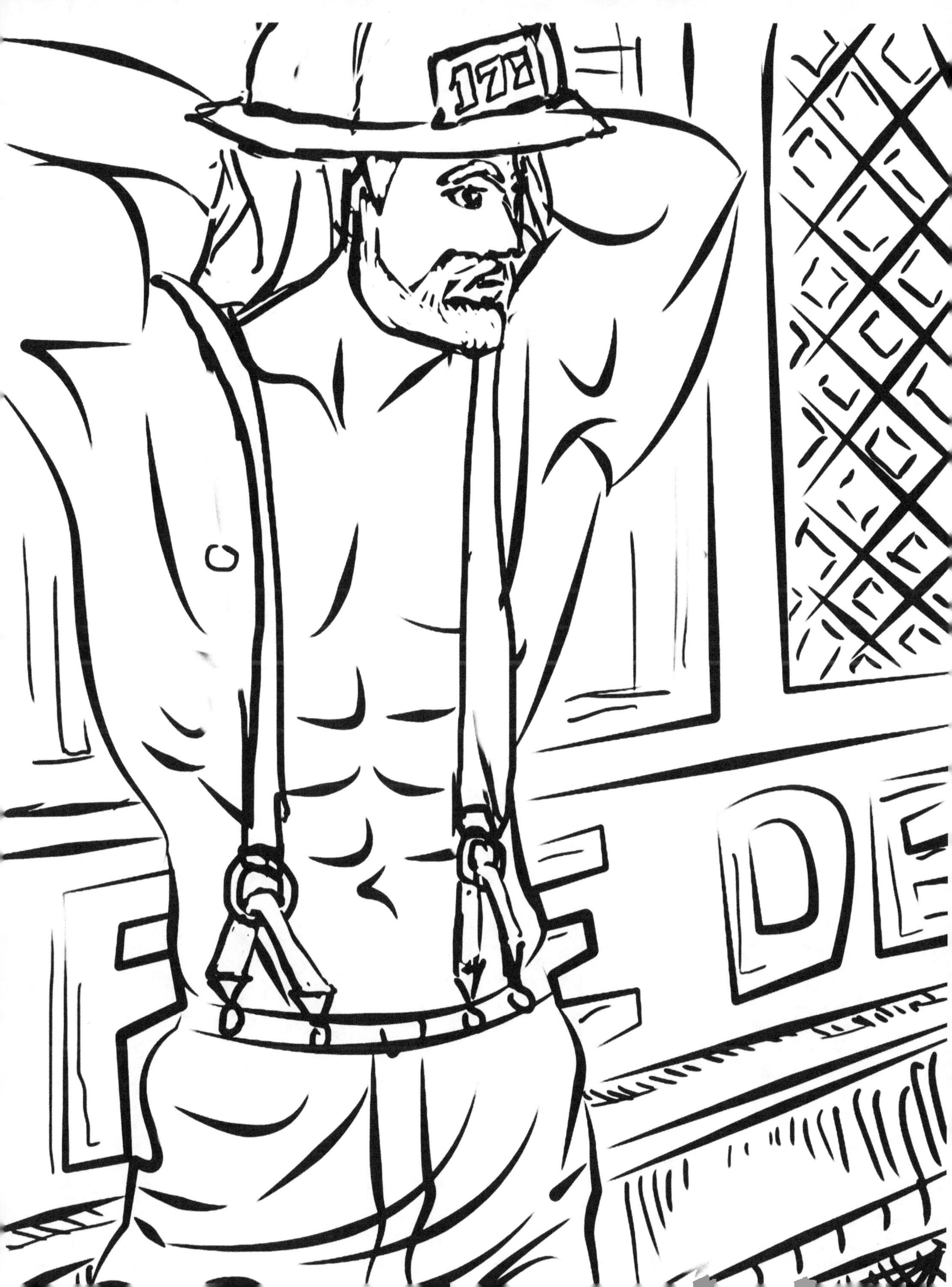

178
DE

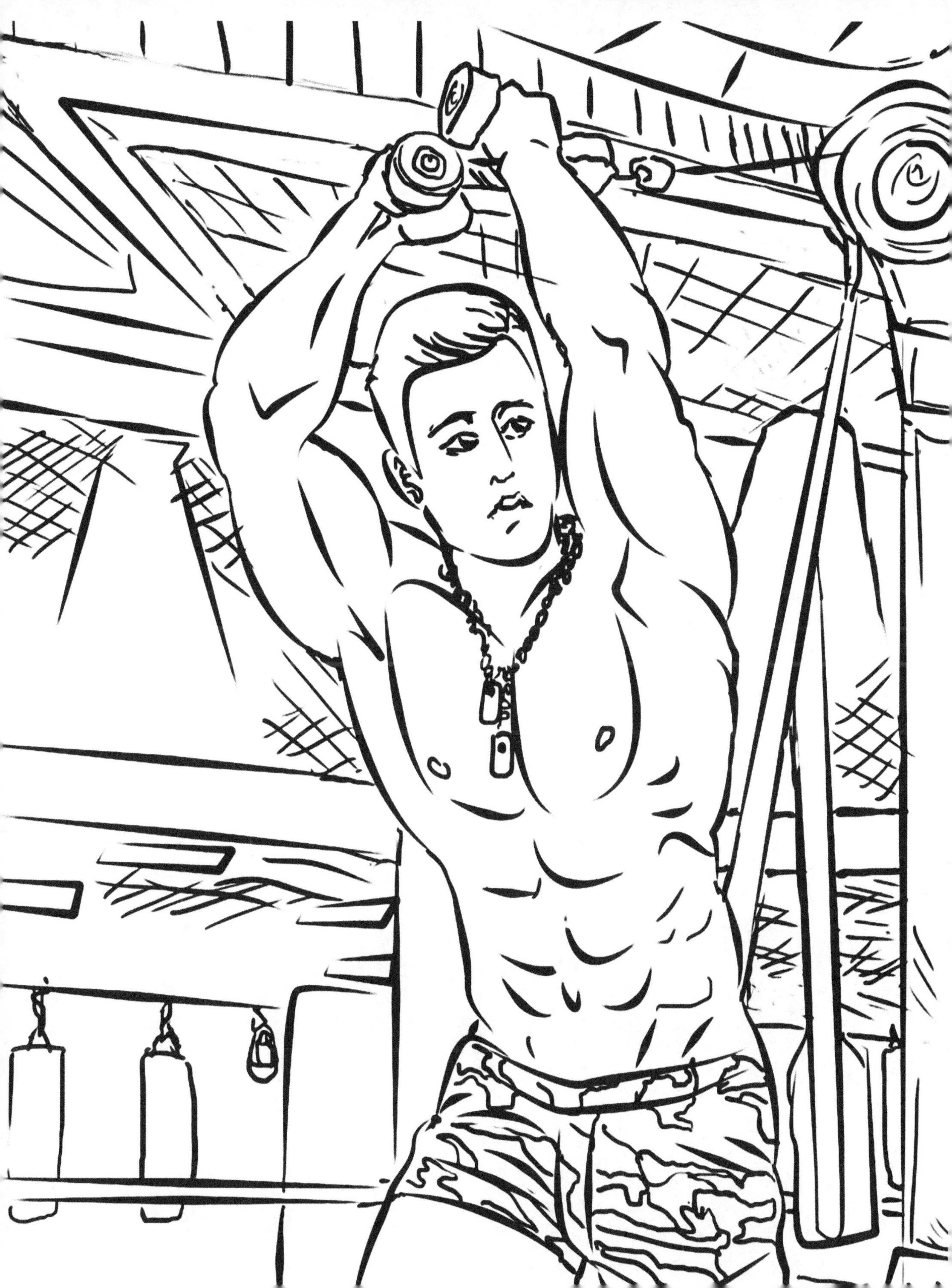

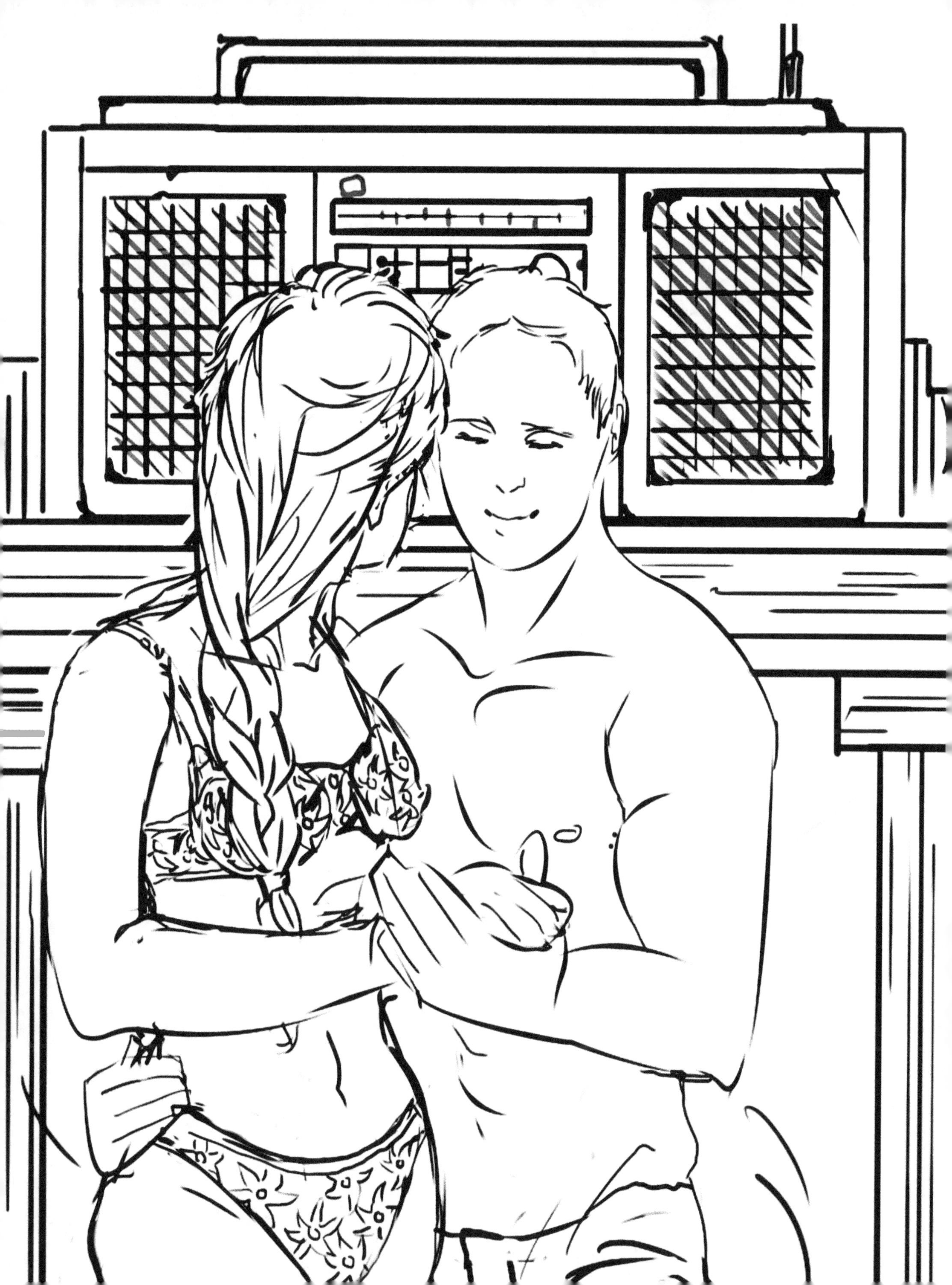

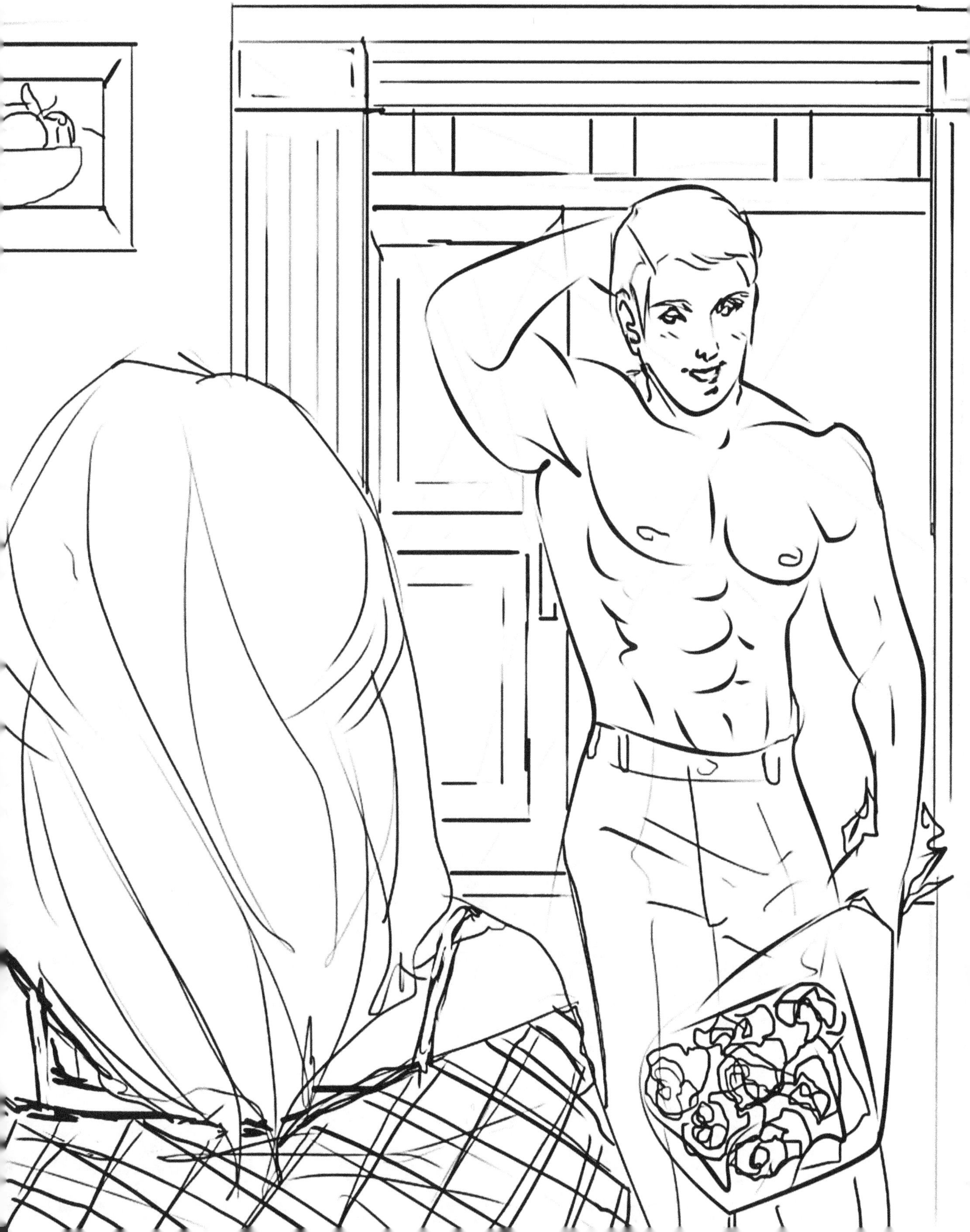

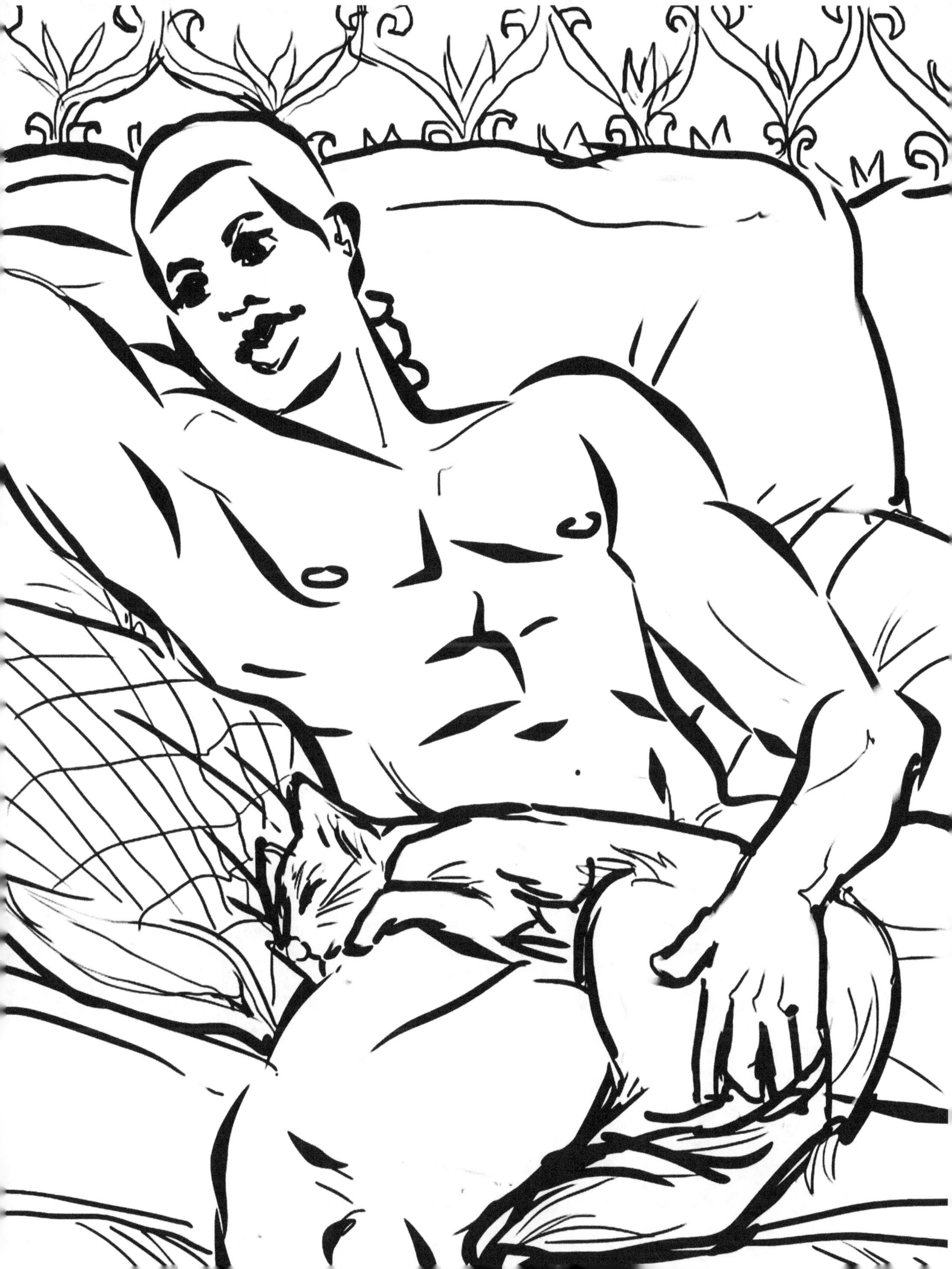

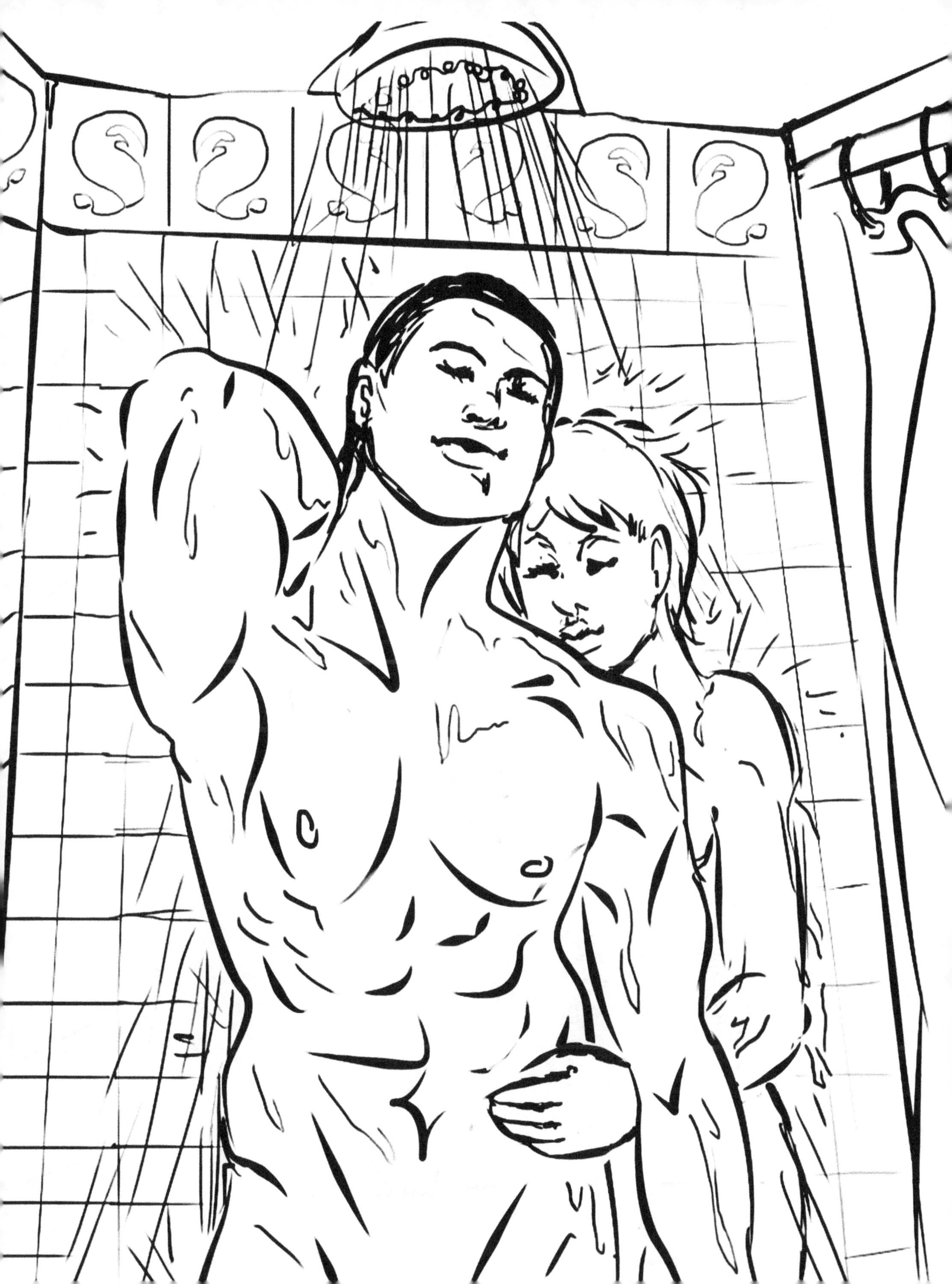

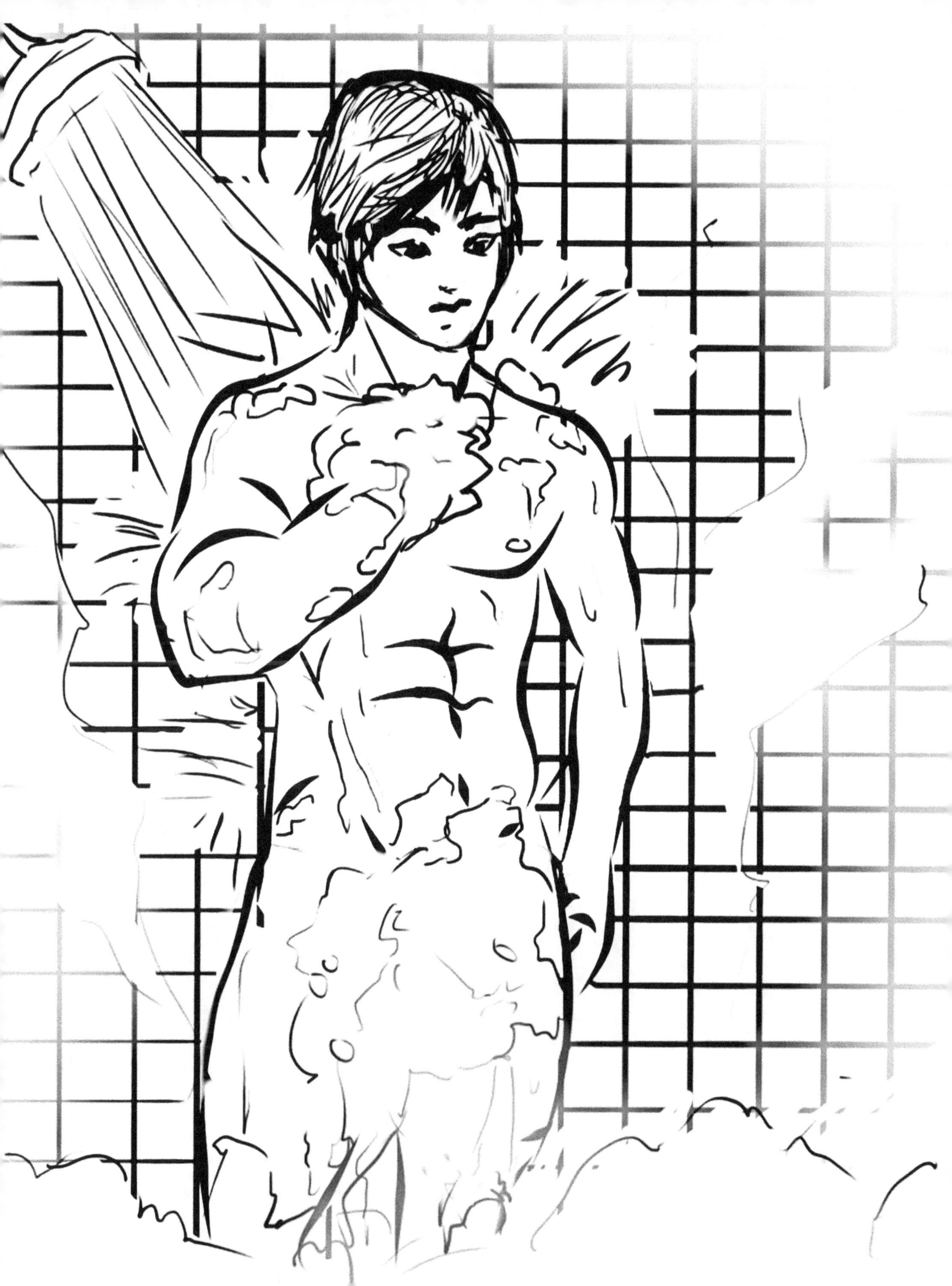

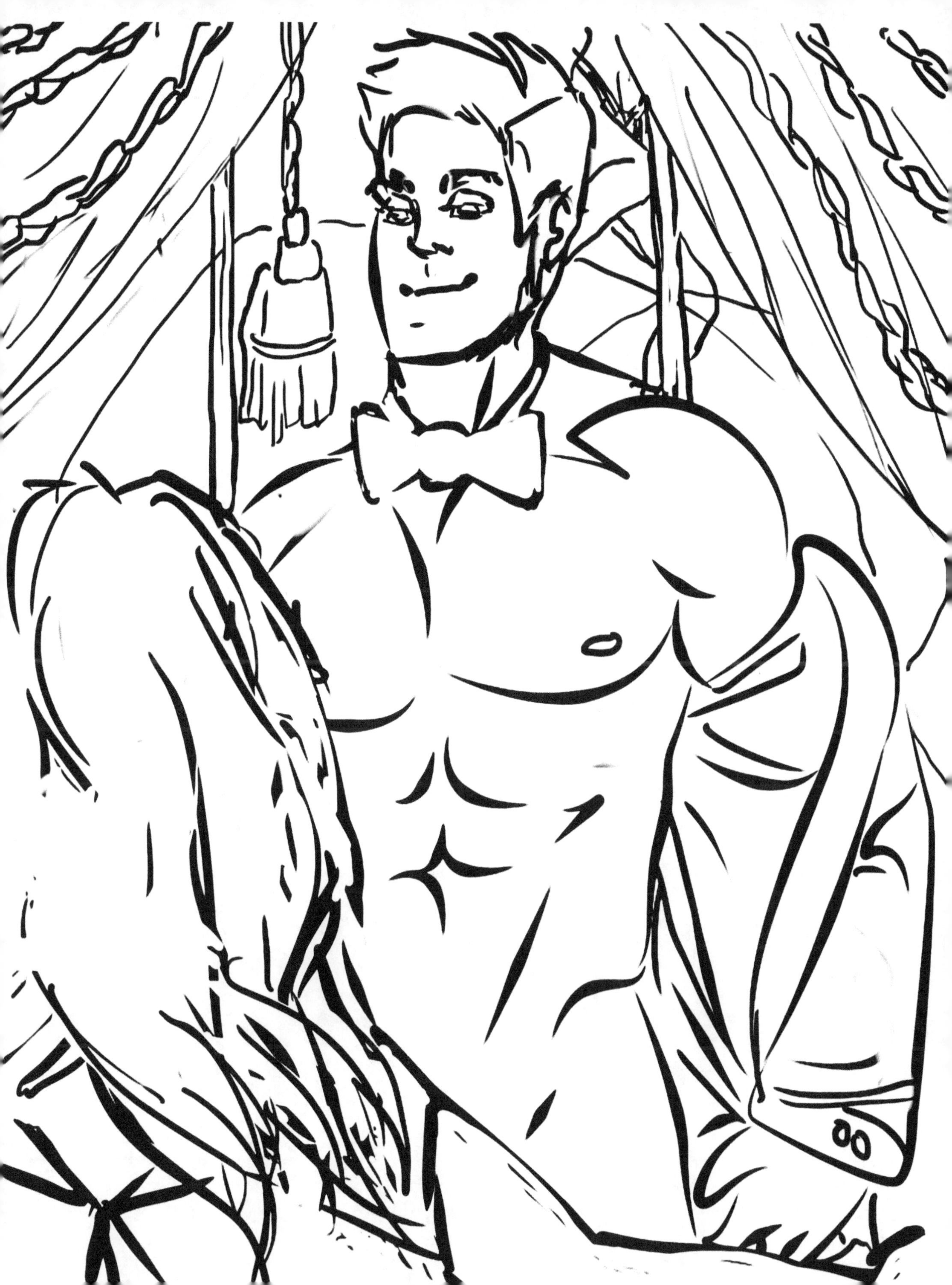

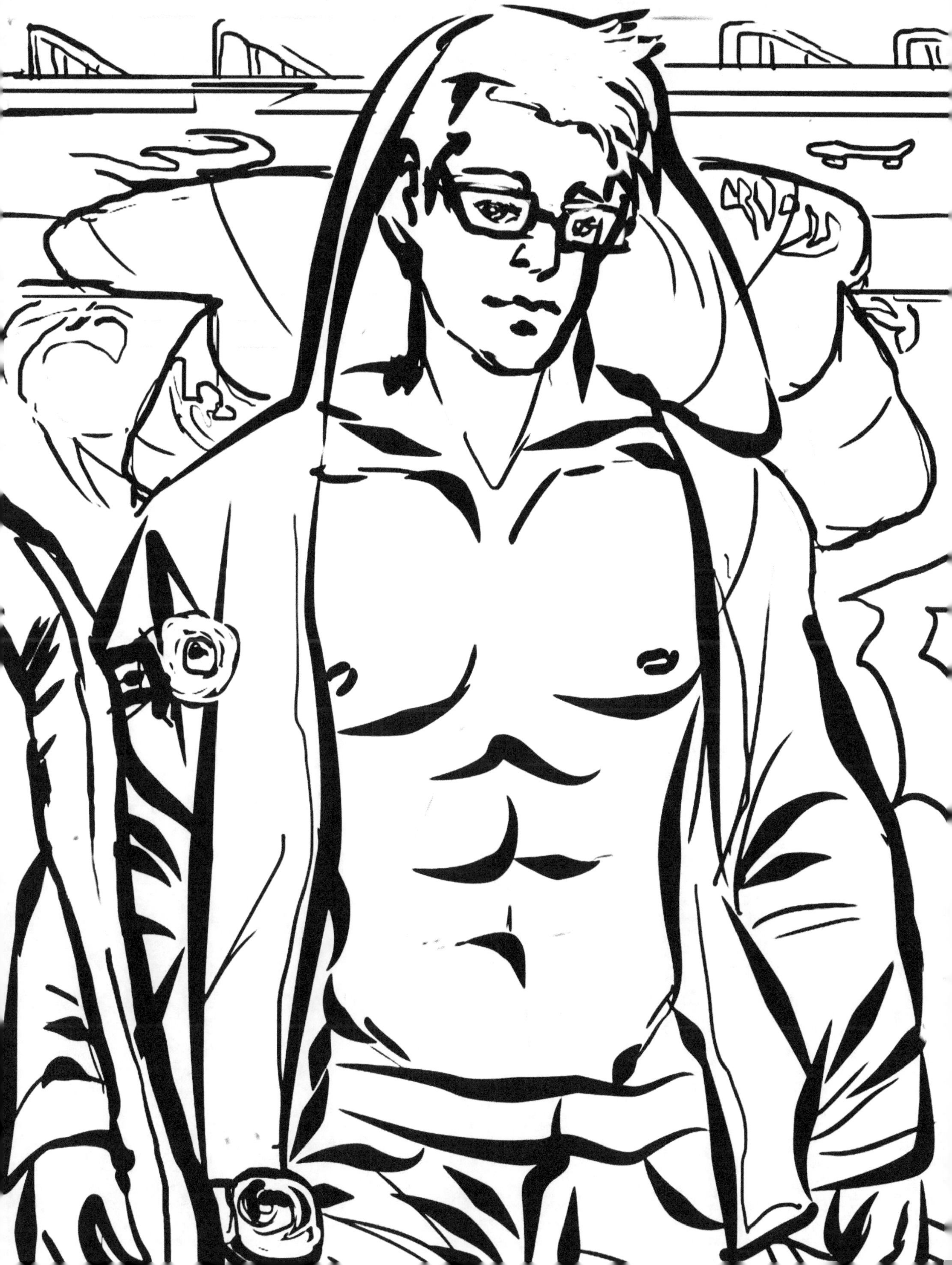

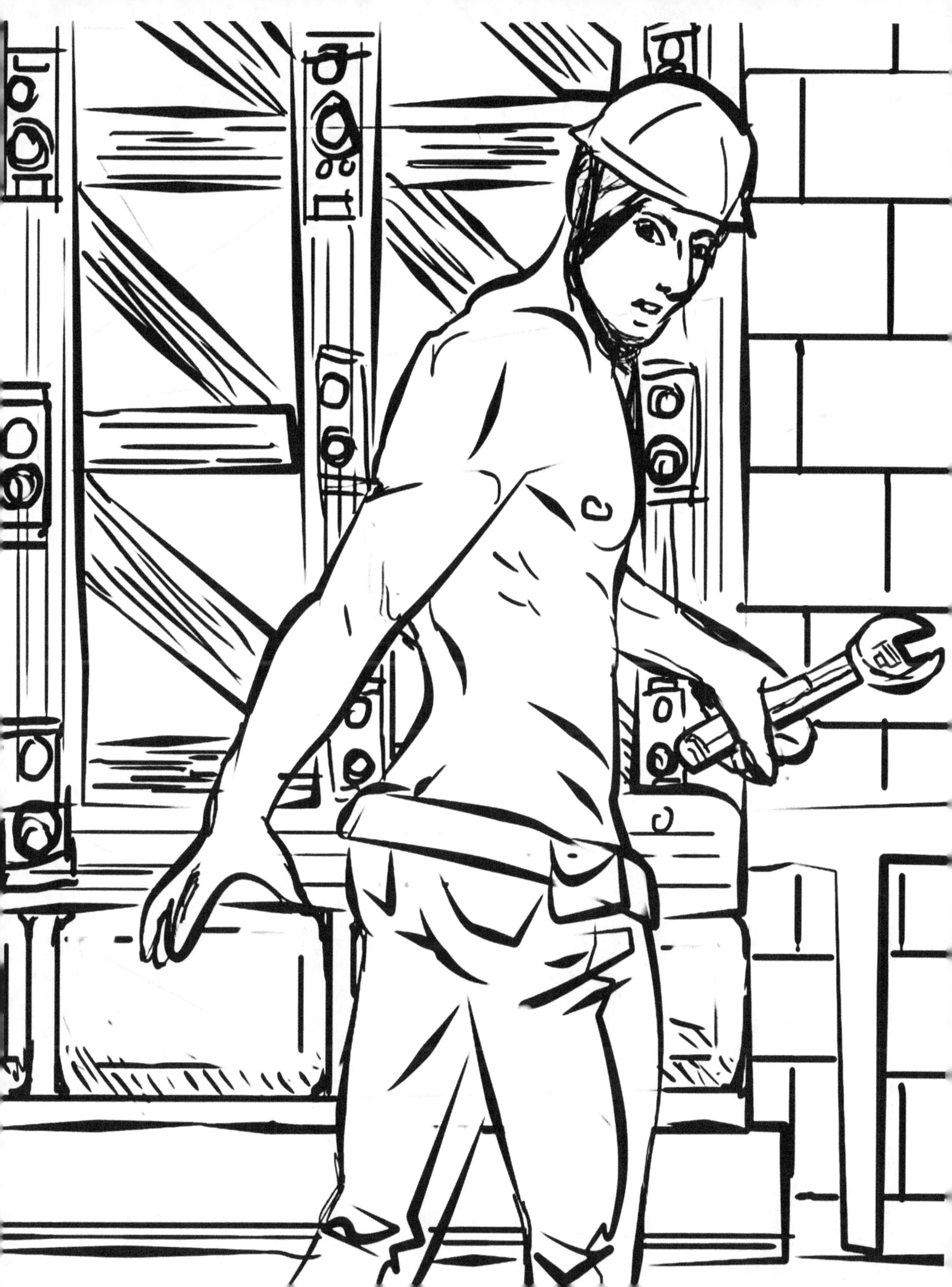

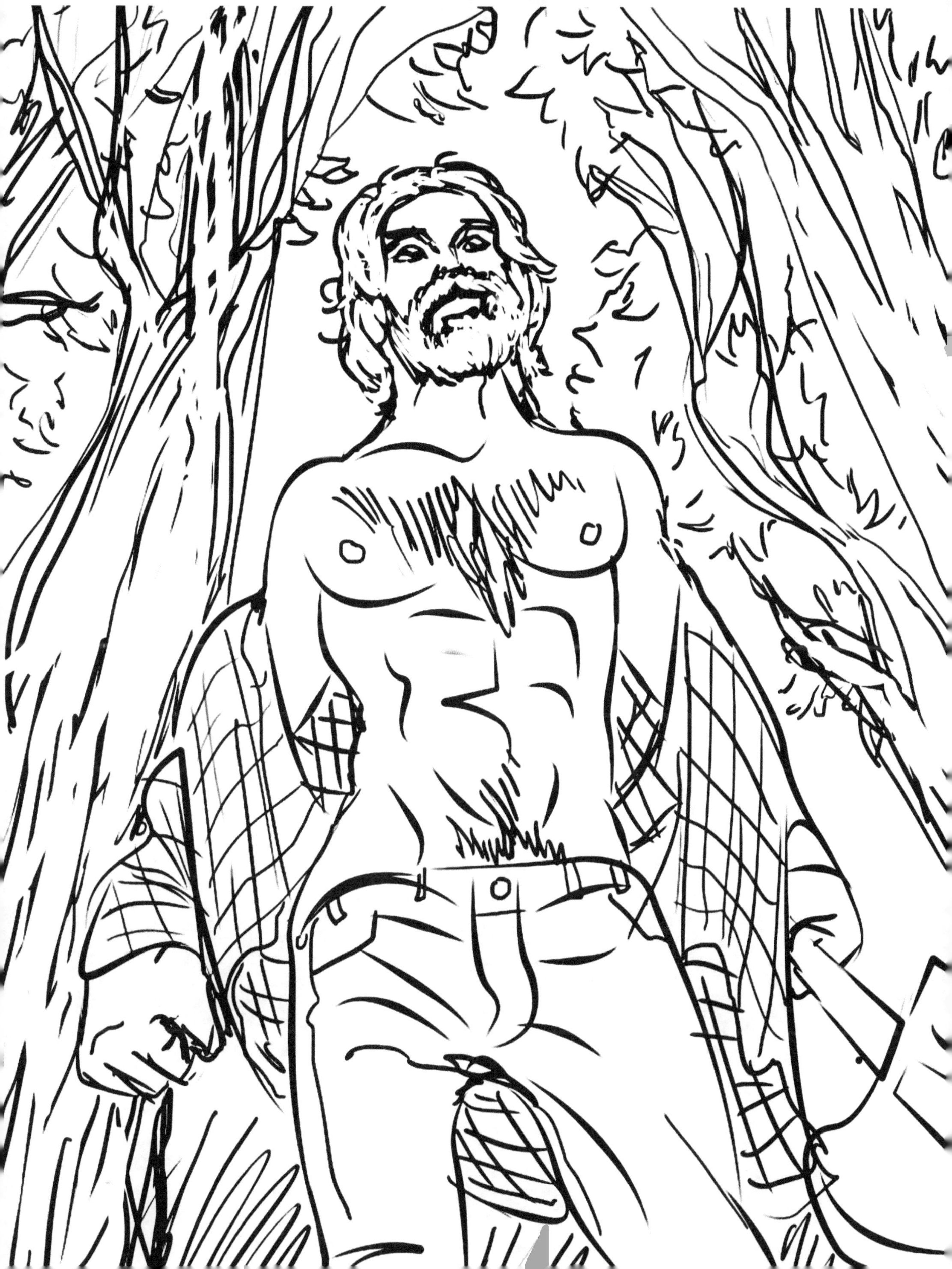

www.ingramcontent.com/pod-product-compliance
Lightning Source LLC
Chambersburg PA
CBHW080649180526
45168CB00008B/3350